To Francesca, Eugenia and Lucía:
the silent companions of this book.

Under the Canopy: Trees around the World © Flying Eye Books 2018.

This is a first edition published in 2018 by Flying Eye Books,
an imprint of Nobrow Ltd. 27 Westgate Street, London E8 3RL.

Illustrations © Cynthia Alonso 2018.

Iris Volant is the pen name of the Flying Eye Books in-house writers.
Text written by Harriet Birkinshaw.

Published in the US by Nobrow (US) Inc.

Printed in Poland on FSC® certified paper.

ISBN: 978-1-911171-42-3

Order from www.flyingeyebooks.com

Iris Volant & Cynthia Alonso

UNDER the CANOPY
Trees around the World

Flying Eye Books

LONDON I NEW YORK

Trees around the World

The TREE of LIFE

From their deep roots in the ground to their branches that sway in the wind, trees have held their place on our planet from the earliest of times. They are the lungs of the world and have inspired our stories, myths and culture. Every climate, every nation has its *tales of trees*, true or legendary, and they help us understand ourselves and the beauty of the world around us. Here are just a few stories about these magnificent plants.

A short tree, reaching no more than 8 to 15 metres high. It is an evergreen, which means it keeps its leaves all year round.

the OLIVE Tree

In ancient Greek myths, the olive tree played a central role. Zeus, the king of the gods, offered a contest between *Athena*, the goddess of wisdom, craft and war, and Poseidon, the god of the sea, for the possession of a city. Each god had to present a gift to the people, and they would choose a winner. Poseidon smashed his three-pronged trident against the hard rock of the Acropolis and a salt spring burst forth; *Athena* produced an olive tree, dangling with abundant fruit. The people chose her olive tree and the city was named Athens, after her. With her gift, she graced the people with a tree that was used for food, heat, medicine, perfume and, of course, olive oil. Today, an olive tree still grows in the same place and is said to have come from the roots of the original tree.

Along the shores of tropical beaches stand coconut trees, growing up to 30 metres high. They produce large oval seeds with hard woody husks, lined with edible white flesh and filled with a milky fluid – coconuts.

The COCONUT Tree

Many Pacific Ocean cultures have myths about the coconut. One of the most well-known is about *Hainuwele*, the Coconut Girl, from Wemale and Alune folklore of the island of Seram in the Maluku islands, Indonesia. Legend tells of a man called Ameta finding a coconut, and planting it. In only a few days the coconut grew into a tall tree, and bloomed. As Ameta climbed the tree to collect the sap, he cut his finger, dripping blood on to the blossom. When he returned days later, he found a girl in place of the blossom. He named her *Hainuwele*, meaning 'coconut branch'. She had a remarkable talent – when she answered the call of nature, she pooed valuables! Sadly, she did not live for long but where the pieces of her body were buried, they grew into various useful plants around the island.

The cherry tree is loved for its bright pink and white blossom.
Growing to no more than 4 metres high, it is a deciduous
tree which means that its leaves fall off in the autumn and
grow again in the spring.

The CHERRY TREE

Picnicking beneath the blossom of a cherry tree is a Japanese tradition known as *hanami*, which means 'flower viewing'. Hundreds of years ago, emperors and members of the Imperial Palace began hosting feasts under the blooming branches. Today, this tradition continues as *hanami* celebrations have become increasingly popular all around the world. It brings many people together to celebrate the beauty of nature. When in bloom, these trees signal the arrival of spring, and their delicate, bright petals light up the world with a sense of hope.

On the island of Madagascar there is a group of baobab trees called the Alley of the Baobabs. These are impressive deciduous trees that reach heights of 30 metres. The large trunks are often hollow, and many birds build their nests inside.

ALLEY OF THE BAOBABS

The baobab is sometimes called 'the upside down tree', because when its leaves have fallen, the branches look like roots sticking up in the air. One bush legend goes that the first baobab tree grew next to a small lake where it saw its reflection in the water. Disgusted at its fat trunk and small tiny leaves, it began to lament its ugly appearance. At last, the gods could take the baobab's complaints no more, so they *uprooted the tree* and replanted it upside down. The baobab could no longer see its reflection or complain, and has since become one of the most useful and helpful trees around. Today it is used by humans for food, medicine and even shelter.

High in the mountains of Lebanon stand the noble evergreen cedar trees, reaching heights of 35 metres. They are conifers, which are trees that bear cones to carry their seeds. Their thin leaves are usually called needles.

the CEDAR Tree

The cedar tree is a symbol of the country of Lebanon, and was used as timber by many kings and pharaohs throughout history. In the Hebrew Bible, *Solomon*, the king of ancient Israel, so admired this tree that he built a palace of cedar. The celebrated temple of Solomon was the first Jewish temple in Jerusalem, and took over 7 years to build. It was built first with stone, then lined with cedar wood which was carved with beautiful open flowers, so that no stone would be seen. Today, although the forest of cedars is greatly diminished, these mighty trees remain immortalized on the country's flag.

THE BANYAN TREE

The banyan tree grows as high as 30 metres. Some species send down a great many shoots from their branches which take root and become trunks.

Wishing trees are recognized as having a special spiritual or religious value. The *Lam Tsuen Wishing Trees* are a popular shrine in Hong Kong. These two banyan trees are situated near the Tin Hau Temple in the 700 year old village of Fong Ma Po. During the lunar new year (traditionally the first day of the month), villagers would write their wishes on special paper tied to an orange before throwing them to hang on the trees. If the paper successfully hung on the trees, it was believed that these wishes would come true. To protect the trees today wishes are no longer hung, but tourists and locals continue to visit and make their own wishes.

Slow-growing and long-living, this medium-sized evergreen can grow to 20 metres in height and live up to 1000 years old. Its dark green leaves are poisonous and in early spring, small yellow flowers peek out.

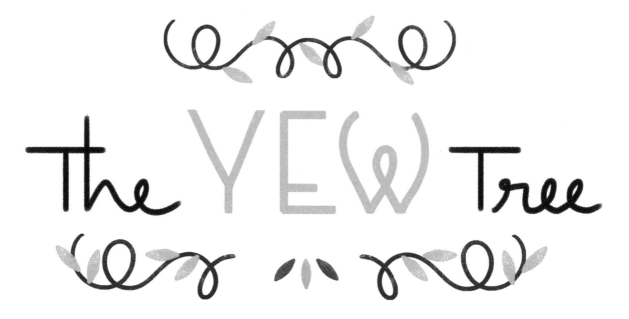

The YEW Tree

The World Tree of Norse mythology, Yggdrasil, is believed to have been a great yew tree. One of its roots sprung from the very centre of the earth and as it rose up, its branches reached out over the whole universe, connecting the nine worlds. On its summit perched an all-seeing eagle, with a hawk sitting between his eyes. A squirrel continually carried news to the eagle, while serpents coiled around the vast trunk wanting to destroy him. The tree was the symbol of all *knowledge and wisdom*, seeking to explain the ties that held the universe together.

A royal forest in Nottinghamshire, England, is home to the famous Major Oak. This deciduous oak tree is between 800 and 1000 years old. Oak trees can grow up to 40 metres tall, with long, lobed leaves and acorns which grow on the long stems.

SHERWOOD FOREST

Many tales have been told of *Robin Hood* and his merry men, who stole from the rich to give to the poor. Robin was a heroic outlaw, skilled swordsman and archer in English folklore. Using the woods as their haven, Robin and his band of men would outwit the rich and resist the unfair rule of the Sheriff of Nottingham. They were able to remain safe and protected by hiding within the trunk of the Major Oak. Even today, oak trees are still seen as a symbol of strength all over the world.

A type of deciduous tree, the elm can reach heights of 35 metres. It has a rough and coarse bark which can be a light or dark grey colour.

The Elm Tree

By the 18th century, thousands of English puritans had settled in the New World, now known as North and South America. The land was still free when an elm sapling took root. Years later, as the tree grew, the city of Boston rose up around it. In 1765, at that very elm tree, settlers staged the first act of defiance against British colonial rule. It became known as 'The Liberty Tree', and was a rallying point for the growing resistance over British rule that led to the American War of Independence 10 years later. For many years, flags bearing the image of this grand elm tree were raised to symbolise the spirit of freedom.

The apple tree is one of the most popular fruit trees in the world. It is a deciduous tree that grows to 10 metres high. When the petals of its blossom fall away, the fruit grows until ripe and falls.

In 1665, mathematician *Isaac Newton* found himself back on his family's farm in Lincolnshire, England. The story goes that one day, while sitting in the orchard, an apple fell on his head. This seemingly small event led him to question why apples always fall straight to the ground. He began to think about why everything always fell down, and not upwards or sideways. Newton realised that there must be a force that draws them to the ground. And so, Newton's theory of gravity was born. A relaxing moment under an apple tree led to the discovery of one of the most famous laws of physics.

Known for the prickly thorns that protect its leaves, the small deciduous hawthorn tree grows to between 5 and 14 metres high.

The HAWTHORN TREE

Growing throughout Europe, the hawthorn tree has inspired many stories in European folklore. In Celtic legends it is known as 'the faery thorn', as it was believed to be the *meeting place of fairies* and marked the opening to the otherworld. It was forbidden to cut down a hawthorn, as bad fortune might befall anyone who did so. Even today, some people still live by this superstition. In Ireland, roads have been diverted to prevent touching a hawthorn tree.

Native to Australia and one of the tallest known flowering plants in the world, the evergreen eucalyptus can grow to over 60 metres tall. Its leaves have a waxy surface and hang down in pairs.

THE EUCALYPTUS TREE

In the mountain ranges west of Sydney, Australia, a blue haze from the oil of the eucalyptus trees rises up, giving the *Blue Mountains* their name. The aboriginal people of Australia have long used the eucalyptus tree for medicinal purposes. The leaves can be infused to help ease body pains, fevers and chills. After British explorer Captain James Cook's third expedition in 1777, the tree was introduced to the rest of the world. Interest in the tree flourished in Europe, but brutal British colonial oppression forever changed the peaceful way of life for the aboriginal people.

In South America is the world's largest tropical rainforest – the Amazon. The lupuna tree is one of the beautiful giants of the rainforest. Its trunk can reach as wide as 10 metres and as tall as 50 metres.

AMAZON RAINFOREST

The lupuna tree (also known as the Kapok) is sacred to the many indigenous tribes still living in the forest. At the widest point on its trunk, a part sticks out which looks similar to the shape of a human stomach. It is believed that the tree contains a spirit known as *the guardian of the rainforest*. Legend tells of a native woman who once urinated on the tree and soon after was inflicted with severe stomach pain. The only way for her to be healed was to beg the tree for forgiveness and drink its sap. The woman fully recovered, having learned the importance of treating the rainforest, and especially the lupuna tree, with great respect.

The ash tree's lance-shaped leaves appear after it flowers, which is unusual in trees. Its many species can grow to between 9 metres and 30 metres tall, and live to 300 years old.

The ASH Tree

The versatility of the ash tree's wood means that it has been used to make everything from handles for tools to the very first lacrosse sticks. These sticks were large spoons made from ash wood, with no netting, carved by the early *Powhatan* tribespeople. The original game could involve hundreds of players and stretch across miles of land. Tribes would often agree to a contest to resolve territorial disputes or settle arguments. Today, some Native American peoples continue their long-standing relationship with the ash tree, using it for firewood and baskets.

The famous weeping willow tree can grow to 20 metres high. They have catkins which are long clusters of flowers without petals. The word 'catkin' comes from the Dutch word 'katteken' meaning 'kitten' because catkins resemble kittens' tails.

The WILLOW Tree

The willow tree originates in China. At the end of the 18th century, the cascading tree was well-known because of the blue and white willow pattern that appeared on tea sets everywhere in England. In order to promote sales of the chinaware, many stories were based on the pattern. One is an Eastern tale of young love forbidden by a tyrannical father. When the beautiful girl falls in love with her father's humble accounting assistant, they are forbidden to marry due to his low social class. After the lovers fail to escape, the gods transform them into *a pair of doves*. At the centre of the ceramic design stands a willow, its leaves waving the lovers on their way.

A slim, dark and mysterious tree, the cypress has been around for thousands of years. It grows to heights of 15 metres and its leaves form in flat sprays and long stalks.

the CYPRESS Tree

In Vincent Van Gogh's famous paintings, 'The Starry Night' and 'The Wheatfield', the vibrant colours of the sky are contrasted against the dark, towering cypress trees. *Van Gogh* was a Dutch post-impressionist artist who lived between 1853 and 1890 and is best-known for his use of colour and for cutting off his own ear in a fit of rage! The cypress tree seemed to speak to him during his most creative and troublesome time. Although he wasn't successful in his lifetime, his paintings, including those of the cypress trees, sell for huge sums of money today and continue to inspire us all.

In Germany, there is a forest so thick with conifer pine and fir trees that the sunlight cannot pierce through the canopy. Fir trees and pine trees can reach heights between 15 and 80 metres.

Black Forest

The Black Forest is the dark playground for numerous legends and myths, including many of the Brothers Grimm's fairy tales. Jacob and Wilhelm Grimm were German writers in the 19th century who collected and published German folklore. Their famous fairy tale of *Hansel and Gretel* is set deep in a wood, much like the Black Forest. A brother and sister are kidnapped by an evil witch who lives in a house made of cake and sweets. When they learn that she wishes to eat them, they cleverly outwit the witch and escape. Set within the hidden shadows of the dark forest, their tale is one of resilience and survival in a place where the imagination can run wild.

The slender and fair silver birch tree can live up to 300 years old and reach heights of 20 metres. It is deciduous and most recognisable by the papery texture of its smooth white and black bark.

the BIRCH Tree

The silver birch tree is usually found in habitats that have been destroyed by fire. In 1888, a great fire spread across the city of Umeå in Sweden, nearly burning it to the ground. It is reported that some birches *halted the spread of the fire*. To protect the city from further fires, the people of the city planted many more and have cared for them ever since. Now called the 'City of Birches', the avenues of Umeå are lined with these elegant trees. In winter, catkins hang down which develop into long crimson flowers in spring.

With large drooping branches, the deciduous horse chestnut tree can grow to 30 metres tall. It has big leaves, long flower spikes and round prickly fruits known as 'conkers'.

The HORSE CHESTNUT Tree

From 1939 to 1945, the second world war raged. In Amsterdam, a young Jewish girl called *Anne Frank* remained hidden from the Nazi German soldiers. In the secret annex of her father's workplace, a single window offered her a small glimpse of the outside world. She often gazed out, taking comfort in the beauty of the white horse chestnut tree in the courtyard. She longed for the freedom of the birds perched on its branches. Although she did not survive the war, her diaries were published afterwards and read across the world. For a short time, the tree offered her hope in a time of great fear.

The acacia tree is native to tropical regions of the world such as those in Australia and Africa. They grow quickly, reaching 12 to 20 metres high, but can only live for 20 to 30 years.

The ACACIA Tree

On the Savannah in Zimbabwe, Africa, you can find the '*whistling acacias*', so named because of their long sharp thorns which make a whistling sound in the wind. Acacia trees provide food and habitats for a variety of animals. Giraffes wrap their long, prehensile tongues between the spines of the thorn and delicately remove the tender tasty leaves. To protect its leaves from giraffes, the tree pumps its leaves with organic chemicals which are poisonous. After a while the giraffe is forced to stop feeding. The chemicals also release a signal into the air that is picked up by other nearby acacia trees. They too pump chemicals into their own leaves knowing that there are hungry giraffes nearby.

The stunning jacaranda tree is native to Central and South America and can grow to 20 metres. When its flowers fall, they form a colourful carpet of purple-blue on the ground.

The JACARANDA Tree

The Guaraní indigenous peoples of Argentina have a story about the origins of the jacaranda tree. In the legend, set in the province now known as Corrientes, a Spanish girl named Pilar fell in love with a native boy called Mbareté. Her father disapproved of the boy, and the lovers fled. But Pilar's angry father sought them out and, in a rage, accidentally killed his daughter and then Mbareté. From where their poor bodies lay, a strong trunk sprung up, full of blue-purple flowers. The lovers had been reborn as the jacaranda tree, as the sturdy trunk was Mbareté and the beautiful flowers were the colour of Pilar's eyes.

Through tales such as this, trees have become symbols of *survival, resilience and rebirth*. Next time you climb high up a tree's trunk, or simply pass one by, perhaps you too will discover your own story and celebrate the magnificence of our silent companions.

WILLOW

SILVER BIRCH

OAK

CYPRESS

APPLE

PINE

OLIVE

ELM

CHERRY

ASH

BANYAN

ACACIA

EUCALYPTUS

HORSE CHESTNUT

COCONUT

FIR

CEDAR

HAWTHORN

BAOBAB

JACARANDA

LUPUNA